Covenant Discipleship
Student's Workbook

Covenant Discipleship Student's Workbook

The Workbook for a new sort of Communicant's Class

Helping Students Understand Faith, Theology, and the Church

By Richard L. Burguet & J. Ed Eubanks, Jr.

Published 2008

Printed by CreateSpace

ISBN 1-440-40449-6

Dedicated to our covenant families:

Burguets:
   Anne, Iain, Elizabeth, Suzanna, Mary Claire, Katie, John, Johnathan, and Mackenzie.

Eubanks's:
   Marcie, Jack, Molly, Abbey, and Caroline.

Thank you for your constant love and support.

Table of Contents

Introduction—Welcome!

Congratulations! You're beginning the Covenant Discipleship Class, a "Communicant's Class" for our church. You might not understand what that means—or even what a "Communicant" is. You might not know why that calls for congratulations, either! Hopefully, as you work through this material, you will understand it more and more.

A Communicant is simply someone who is a member of the church (we'll talk about why they are called Communicants later!). By beginning this class, you have begun a process that, if everything goes according to plan, will result in you becoming a Communicant—a full-fledged member of the church. This process will do three important things to lead you toward that result: it will help you understand faith and how it applies to you; it will talk about what Christians believe and some things that make our church Presbyterian; and it will help you to understand how our church works and how you can be an important part of it. Joining a church is a big deal, and we want you to consider it carefully; this is a decision that will make a big difference in your life.

What is church membership? What do you have to do to be a member of the church? In our church, the answer to this question seems pretty simple. According to the our denomination's Book of Church Order (a book which describes the way our church is organized) all that is required for church membership is that a person make "a profession of faith in Christ, have been baptized, and have been admitted by the Session to the Lord's Table."

But what does all of this mean? These requirements really do not give us a clear understanding of what church membership is, unless you understand each of those different parts. What is a profession of faith? How about baptism? What is the Session? What is the Lord's Table, and what does it mean to be admitted to it? Do you meet these requirements, or not?

All of these questions, and a lot of others, are answered through this class. If there is anything about the church that you don't understand, we'll try to answer it in the

Covenant Discipleship class. This is a nine-lesson program, with each lesson covering a different part of the information you need to understand what it means to be a member of the church. The first six lessons are done at home-you'll do these with your parents. The last three lessons will be taught by the Pastor and the Elders. We'll use this workbook for both parts of the class, so it will be very important to you.

Here is the basic schedule of the nine-lesson Covenant Discipleship Class:	
Lesson 1	Faith and Its Foundations: What is Faith and Why Have It?
Lesson 2	Understanding Your Faith: Up Close and Personal
Lesson 3	Basic Training: a Look at the Basics of What We Believe
Lesson 4	Why Do We Baptize Babies? And Other Good Questions…
Lesson 5	The Church: Isn't It Just a Building?
Lesson 6	Getting Down to Business: the Organization of the Church
Lesson 7	Faith and You: Review of Weeks 1 & 2
Lesson 8	What Presbyterians Believe: Review of Weeks 3 & 4
Lesson 9	We Are the Church Together: Review of Weeks 5 & 6

This workbook is designed to be used by you, and your parents will help you go through it. Your parents have a similar book that will help them help you with some of the stuff that's in here— stuff that you might have some trouble with as you're working on it. There are a lot of questions that you should try to answer as completely as you can, but don't worry about things like grammar or complete sentences. You only need to write down as much as you need to remember what the right answer is, if you ever read over this book again later. The important thing is that you understand what is being talked about, and that you ask questions about things you don't understand. Don't be afraid to ask questions-nobody else knew the answers before asking questions, either!

This is an exciting time for you! Are you ready? Then let's go!

Lesson 1: Faith and Its Foundation

What Is Faith, and Why Have It?

In the first lesson, we'll look at what faith is and how it is developed. We'll also look at the "foundations" of faith-what makes a person's faith believable and strong. And we'll talk about the Bible, and begin to look at how God relates to man.

Psalm 127
A SONG OF ASCENTS, OF SOLOMON.
¹Unless the LORD builds the house,
They labor in vain who build it;
Unless the LORD guards the city,
The watchman keeps awake in vain.
²It is vain for you to rise up early,
To retire late,
To eat the bread of painful labors;
For He gives to His beloved even in his sleep.
³Behold, children are a gift of the LORD,
The fruit of the womb is a reward.
⁴Like arrows in the hand of a warrior,
So are the children of one's youth.
⁵How blessed is the man whose quiver is full of them;
They will not be ashamed
When they speak with their enemies in the gate.

Section 1: What is this faith stuff?

So, What is faith? In the Bible, Hebrews chapter 11, verse 1 tells us. Look that up, and copy it here:

Now, what does this mean? Re-write this verse in words that describe faith as it applies to you. You might want to discuss it with your parents before you're finished.

That same chapter of Hebrews discusses a lot of people who are called "heroes of the faith" in the Bible. How did these people show their faith, and why was it important for them? Discuss some of them with your parents, and write down what you discuss.

Abel (Genesis 4:3-15):

Enoch (Genesis 5:21-24):

Noah (Genesis 6:9-7:22):

Abraham (Genesis 12:1-5; 21:1-7; 22:1-19):

Isaac (Genesis 27:1-39):

Jacob (Genesis 48:8-22):

Joseph (Genesis 50:24-26):

Moses' parents (Exodus 2:1,2):

Moses (Exodus 2:11-15; 12:31-33; 12:1-16):

Israelites (Exodus 13:17-14:31):

Joshua— Walls of Jericho (Joshua 5:13-6:27):

Rahab (Joshua 2:1-24):

How does the Bible define faith? How do the examples in the Bible demonstrate for us faith in God? Why is faith important for us? Discuss these questions with your parents.

Section 2: The foundations of faith

A lot of people believe in a lot of different things; some people have faith in other religious beliefs, like Judaism (the Jewish religion) or Islam (the Muslim religion). Others believe in things like ghosts, witchcraft, or reincarnation—not exactly organized religions, but still significantly different beliefs from Christianity.

It is very important that we understand why our faith is valid, and why it is believable. In getting this understanding, we'll also begin to see why other religious beliefs do not have as much foundation as Christianity.

Read Matthew 7:24-27. What do these verses say about the importance of a strong foundation for faith?

What do you think makes Christianity a faith with a strong foundation?

Section 3: The Bible— a strong foundation

The Bible is the foundation for Christianity—and it is a strong one. As Christians, we give the Bible a lot of attention and emphasis, because of what we believe about it.

What do we believe about the Bible? List some things that you think Christians believe about the Bible.

What does the Bible say about itself? Look up the following sets of verses, and write down what you understand them to be saying.
Leviticus 1:1-17:

Deuteronomy 18:18,19; 31:9-13:

Jeremiah 1:1-19:

II Thessalonians 2:13:

II Timothy 3:14,17:

II Peter 3:16:

What does Jesus say about the Bible? Look up the following sets of verses, and write down what you understand them to be saying.
Matthew 5:18; 24:35:

John 10:35:

Section 4: The Bible, part 2

In the Church, we talk about the whole Bible being inspired by God, and about the Bible being infallible, or "not able to fail." This means that the writing of every part of the Bible is inspired by, or directed by, God. God gave His words to the human authors so that when they wrote the books that make up the Bible, they wrote only what God wanted them to write, and they wrote everything God wanted them to write. This also means that, like God, the Bible is not able to fail-what it says is never wrong, and it is always everything that needs to be said. The Bible, as God's word, is all that we need for our growth and development as Christians.

Discuss These Questions With Your Parents:

How do we know that the whole Bible is inspired by God?

How do we know that the Bible is infallible—unable to fail?

What is the Bible useful for in our lives? How can we use the Bible to understand God?

Why do we consider the Bible to be a solid foundation for our faith? What do you believe about the Bible?

Section 5: How God relates to us

Everyone is in a relationship with God. There is no one that you know, and no one in the world, who does not have a relationship with God. Here's the key question: is each relationship a right relationship, or a wrong one? Your relationship with God is important, and you should know whether or not it is a right or wrong relationship.

What makes a relationship with God a right relationship? That's a good question. The answer is in the Bible—that is part of why it is important that we understand the value and truth of the Bible. If what the Bible says is true, then what the Bible says about our relationship with God is also true. So what does the Bible say about our relationship with God?

Begin with Romans 1:18-32. What does this text say about man, and how man and God relate?

What things do you know about yourself, and others, that affects your relationship with God according to these verses?

Read Genesis chapter 3. How did the world get this way?

In what condition do we say that the world is, because of these verses? What parts of the world are not considered to be in this condition?

Lesson 1 Summary

We've come a long way this week! Let's look back over what we've learned and write down a few summaries about it.

What is faith? Of the "heroes of the faith," who did you learn the most from? Why?

Why is it important to have a strong foundation for our faith? What is that foundation?

What two words do we use to describe the Bible? What do they mean? How do we know that these words accurately describe the Bible?

What condition is the world in right now? Why is it in that condition? Does man know that God exists?

Let's memorize a verse from the Bible to close this week out: it's one of the ones that you looked up during your study. Memorize II Timothy 3:16.

Lesson 2: Understanding Your Faith

Up Close and Personal

In this lesson, we'll look at different things about your own faith, and the faith of other people that you know, like your parents or other members of the church. We'll continue to talk about the world we live in, and how God relates to it. We'll also look at the basics of the Gospel, and discuss salvation, which is the result of the faith that we discussed last week.

Section 1: God's relationship to the world, continued: God's righteousness

Man is sinful-that is, he is not able to always do everything that is good and right. Remember in section 5 last week, we talked about how the whole world is "fallen" and is affected by sin, and how all people are considered sinful or unable to do what is right.
How does this change how we relate to God? Let's find out.

Read Genesis 2:15-17. What did God command? What did Adam do, in spite of God's command?

What would happen if God did not keep His word? Would God be a god who we could trust? What must happen in response to Adam's disobedience if God is to remain "just"—that is, trustworthy?

Read Romans 6:23. Is the same thing true for us today? What are "wages?" What wages have you, and everyone around you, earned?

Section 2: God's relationship to the world, part 3: mercy and grace

Man is sinful and deserving of adequate punishment. God is just and trustworthy and therefore must punish man. But God, in His great love for us, had a plan full of mercy and grace—a plan for our salvation. These are concepts we will focus on today.

What is "mercy?" Discuss this with your parents. What does the word mean? How do we see it in God's plan for our salvation? Read John 3:16-18, and 3:36. How does God maintain both mercy and justice?

What is "grace?" Discuss this word with your parents. How do we see God's grace in Jesus? How do mercy and grace work together for our salvation?

Talk about Jesus, and who he was, with your parents. Why was Jesus the only one who could provide salvation for us? What four things about Jesus' life are needed for that salvation to be complete?

Section 3: Jesus OUR salvation

So, God in His wisdom and love provided a way for man to be saved from His judgment. But, in order for that to happen, there must be an identification with Jesus—we must be adopted into the family of God. If we have faith in God, we will have these things. These two concepts-identification and adoption—will be our topics for this section.

Read Matthew 27:3-5. What does Judas do in this passage? Is what Judas did enough for salvation in Jesus Christ?

Now read Mark 14:66-72. What was the difference between Peter's response to his own sin and Judas' response? What do we call the response that Peter had? Have you made a similar response for your own sin? Describe that response.

Read Galatians 2:20. Discuss this verse with your parents. Do you understand identification with Jesus Christ? Do you have a similar identification as what the apostle Paul describes here? Describe your identification with Jesus Christ.

Now read John 1:12-13. Discuss the idea of "believing in him" with your parents. Do you have the right to be called a child of God? What does this mean for you?

Section 4: What is a testimony?

The word "testimony" is a legal term, used by lawyers and in courts. It means "evidence" or "a statement given under oath." When someone has seen something happen that is against the law, they are asked to give testimony about what they saw.

We use the idea of a testimony in the church, too. When someone has seen God at work, then their description of that work is their testimony. A lot of people talk about what they have learned from reading the Bible recently, or about something that they learned from a sermon or Sunday School lesson—those are testimonies. Some people will describe how God has changed their heart about something or someone—that is a testimony.

All Christians have a testimony; if a person has the identification with Jesus Christ that we talked about in the last section— if they have been adopted into the family of God—then they can give testimony to how God was at work in their lives in this way. This testimony is an account of salvation, a description of how a person came to understand that Jesus is their Savior and Lord.

Do you have a testimony? In the last section we discussed how you know if you are a Christian- how to know if you have been adopted into God's family. If you know that you are a Christian, then you have a testimony. This is an important thing to have—you will be asked to give testimony to your salvation in Jesus Christ in order to join the church. We'll spend the rest of this section and all of the next discussing your testimony.

What is your testimony? Discuss with your parents each of the following topics:
- What is your understanding of your need for salvation?
- When did you first understand this need?
- What have you done in response to your understanding of this need for salvation?
- Do you believe that God is at work in your life?
- What are you doing to help your faith to grow?
- What are you doing to put your faith into action?

Make notes here:

Section 5: Your testimony

It is helpful to have your testimony written down in some form, so that if or when you need to remind yourself of God's work in your life, you can do that easily. Your written testimony does not need to be in any special format: you do not need to worry about correct grammar or complete sentences. You can write it as an "outline" or as a poem if you want to, or you can just write it as a letter to yourself or someone else. The important thing is that you try to write it out.

Write out your testimony here.

Lesson 2 Summary

What does it mean for God to be just?

How does God show mercy and grace to us? What significant thing do we have because of that?

What does it mean to have "identification" with Jesus Christ?

How do people become adopted into the family of God?

What is a testimony? Why is it important to understand yours?

This week's memory verse: 2 Corinthians 5:21

Lesson 3: Basic Training

A Look at the Basics of What We Believe

Because you are moving toward joining the church, it is important that you understand the basics of what a Presbyterian church believes. As Christians, we call our beliefs theology: that word simply means "the study of God." Understanding the basic theology of the church is essential for all Christians, and that's the purpose of this section.

We've already talked about sin, mercy, grace, God's righteousness, and our salvation—these are all a part of theology! If you understand these concepts, then you already know a pretty good amount of theology.

There are some other areas of theology that are important for us to understand: God's covenants with man, justification, and sanctification. These things will be our topics for this lesson.

Section 1: God's covenants with man

You've probably heard this word at some point: covenant. But what is a covenant? A covenant can be defined very simply: it is an agreement that binds or obligates two parties. This is a very common thing—two students agree to meet at the movie theater for a show: this is a covenant. Two adults commit to each other for marriage: this is a covenant. A man signs a contract saying he will work for a certain company or individual: this is a covenant. Anytime two "parties"-that is, two individuals or groups—make some sort of agreement that both are committed to, it can be called a covenant.

When it comes to a covenant with God, things change a little bit. How do they change? Think back over what you have learned so far, and talk this over with your parents. Write your thoughts here.

Section 2: God's covenants with man, part 2

God has made covenants with mankind over time, and these covenants are important for us to understand. There are two, and they each go by several names; we'll use the most common names. They are: the Covenant of Works, and the Covenant of Grace. Each of these is significant for our faith, so we'll look at each one individually.

Let's turn to the Scriptures to learn about them. You should discuss these questions with your parents as you go through them. We'll start with the Covenant of Works.

Read Genesis 1:26-31. What things did God say about his creation called man? Write down each thing that God said about man.

Read Genesis chapter 2. What do we learn about the Garden of Eden? Particularly, what is said about Adam and his wife in the garden?

What responsibilities did Adam and his wife have in order to keep their covenant with God? What would happen to them if they did not keep their responsibilities?

Read Genesis chapter 3. Did Adam and Eve keep their responsibilities? How did their actions effect their covenant with God? Discuss with your parents God's mercy and grace in relation to this covenant.

Section 3: God's covenants with man, part 3

We've talked about the Covenant of Works, now we'll discuss the Covenant of Grace.
Adam and Eve did not keep their covenant with God, and the Covenant of Works was finished. The good news is that God had another covenant. While the Covenant of Works said, "do this and you will live" (see Gen. 2:17, Rom. 10:5), the Covenant of Grace was given to man even though he was unable to keep any command or covenant—simply by God's grace.
Let's discuss it.

What does the term "redemption" mean? Think about what happened during the Covenant of Works, and how that effects you. What need is there for redemption after this?

Read John 3:16,17, and John 10:17,18. What do these sets of verses say about God's plans for the redemption of man?

Discuss the Covenant of Grace with your parents. In your own words, what is the Covenant of Grace?

Because of God's eternal plan to save His elect, the Covenant of Grace is possible. As soon as the Covenant of Works was broken—and man was fallen—the Covenant of Grace became effective, even though it was not stated as such until later in the Scriptures.

Look back over the "heroes of the faith" list. How was God's grace at work in the lives of these people?

Look at Leviticus chapters 4 and 5. What was it that removed the guilt and provided forgiveness for the sins of the Israelites? How did this work?

Read Jeremiah 31:31-34. Discuss with your parents how the covenant mentioned in this passage is a part of the Covenant of Grace. How is this part of the Covenant of Grace fulfilled?

Describe how the two covenants we've studied work together. How has God provided for His people through covenants? What comfort can we know from these covenants?

Section 4: Justification

Here's another word that you may be familiar with: justification. This word is very important for you, because it describes something that may have already happened in your life. Justification is the first part of a two-part process that is the central aspect of our lives as Christians.

If you look at the word justification, you might notice that there are several other words that look or sound similar. What words can you think of that are this way? Discuss with your parents how these words are related to the word justification.

Read Romans chapter 5. What does the apostle Paul say about justification in this chapter? Based on this reading, write what you think justification is in your own words.

Describe what the significance of justification is to a Christian. Has justification occurred in your life? Talk about this with your parents, and write how justification affects you.

Section 5: Sanctification

If justification is the first part of a two-part process, the sanctification is the second part of that process. While justification happens only once and lasts forever, sanctification is an ongoing activity that does not end until death—at that point, glorification takes over-that's when Christians no longer struggle or have to deal with sin any more.
Sanctification is really great, because it is a way for God to continually care for us as His children, and it enables us to know Him more deeply. Let's look at what sanctification is:

Read Romans chapter 6. In partnership with chapter 5 and justification, what does chapter 6 say about sanctification? Based on your reading in chapter 6, write a definition of sanctification in your own words.

What events and activities occur in your life that are a part of sanctification? Discuss this with your parents, and write your list below.

Lesson 3 Summary

What is a covenant? Name the two covenants we discussed.

What covenants provide for our salvation? How do they do that?

Give a definition of the words justification and sanctification.

What is the difference between justification and sanctification?

Memory verses: Romans 6:14,15

Lesson 4: Why Do We Baptize Babies?

And Other Good Questions…

Last week, we covered the basic theology that the Presbyterian church believes. The concepts of covenants, justification, and sanctification are the building blocks of our theology.

In this lesson, we'll discuss more theology; there are some areas of theology that are particular to Presbyterians, and are sometimes real "hot potato" issues. They are predestination, the sacraments.

Section 1: Predestination

Discuss the word predestination with your parents. What words do you recognize as being similar words to this one? What do those other words mean?

Read Romans 8:28-30 and Ephesians 1:3-8. What do these verses say about predestination? Who is predestined? What else happens to those who are predestined?

Read John 15:16. What does Jesus say that relates to predestination? What does this mean about the salvation that Christians have?

Some Christians have a difficult time accepting what the scripture says about predestination. Why do you think this is the case? What might stand in the way of easy acceptance of this concept?

Section 2: The Sacraments, part 1

What is a sacrament? The dictionary says it is simply a religious ritual, but it is more than that. A sacrament is something that is representative of God's covenant with His chosen people. In the Old Testament, some of the sacraments were circumcision (see Genesis chapter 17), the Passover (see Exodus 12), and the sacrifices offered (see Leviticus chapters 1-5). For the New Testament, and for the church today, there are two: Baptism and Communion (or the Lord's Supper). We'll look at what these mean, and why they are important. We'll also look at what particular ways of practicing these sacraments are, according to our theology, most true to the Bible.

Read Genesis 17. What was Abraham commanded to do, as a sign of the covenant between him and God? When was he required to do this? What did this mean? Discuss this with your parents.

Read Galatians chapter 2, and 3:26-29. Are we still required to do what Abraham was required to do? Why or why not? Discuss this with your parents.

What happens today to serve as a sacrament in the same way that circumcision did for Abraham? How does this serve as the substitute for circumcision? Discuss this with your parents.

In your own words, describe what baptism is, and what significance it has. Also talk about why we baptize infants as well as adults in the presbyterian church.

Section 3: The Sacraments, part 2

We've talked about baptism, and how it serves as a sacrament. Now let's talk about communion, or the Lord's Supper.

Read Exodus 12:5-13. What was the Passover? What significance did it have for the Israelites? What did it symbolize for them?

Now read Matthew 26:26-29. How does communion replace the Passover for Christians in the New Testament and today? Discuss this with your parents.

Read John 6:48-58 and I Corinthians 11. What do the wine (or grape juice) and bread stand for in communion? What is the purpose of taking communion for Christians today? Discuss this with your parents.

Read I Corinthians 11:27-30 again. What does Paul (the writer) warn Christians about in this passage? What does this tell you about how you should approach the sacraments, especially communion?

In your own words, describe what communion is, and why it is important for Christians.

Lesson 4 Summary

What is predestination? Does it apply to you?

What is a sacrament? How is it significant for Christians?

Why do we baptize babies?

Is the Lord's Supper important?

Memory verse: Galatians 3:28.

Lesson 5: The Church
Isn't It Just a Building?

Since you're working toward joining the church, it is important to think about the different things that make up the church. We've already talked about the church as a place of faith, and we've discussed some of the important theology of the church. In this lesson, we want to take a look at the church itself, in a variety of ways. We'll look at the church as a universal body of people, and as a local institution. We'll look at how the church is involved in the lives of others. And, we'll look at how you fit into the church, and some of the ways you can be involved in the church as a member.

Section 1: The church universal and the church particular

Many people think of the church as a particular place—maybe a building they worship in, or in some cases another place like a clearing by a lake, or a mountainside. Some other people think of the church as an organization, not very different from the Boy Scouts or the YMCA. But is the church only a building, or only an organization? Or is it much more than this?
Let's look to the Bible, and see what it tells us about the church.

Read Hebrews 11:1-12:3. Remember the Heroes of the Faith? What does 12:1 say about them? How does this apply to the church? Discuss the idea of a "universal church" with your parents.

Read 1 Corinthians 1:2,3; Galatians 1:2,3; Revelation 2:1,8,12,18; Revelation 3:1,7,14. What do each of these verses have in common? What is different about each? Discuss with your parents the idea of a "particular" church.

Section 2: The church ministers to others

What are some of the ways that the church is involved in the world? What are some of the ministries that the church has to those who are a part of it? This section will look at these issues.

List all of the ministries of our church— ways that the church effects the lives of other people-that you can think of. Don't forget to include all sorts of people, of all ages.

There are some ministries of the church that work toward sharing the Gospel (which we discussed earlier) with people who do not know the Gospel; we'll call these Outreach or Evangelism ministries. Can you think of any of these in our church? List them here.

There are some ministries which have the purpose of helping people to understand the Bible and what it instructs us to know and do. We'll call these Teaching ministries. Do you know of any of these at our church? List them here.

There are ministries that are for the purpose of helping people who are in need in some way; we'll call these Benevolence ministries. Which of these do you know about in our church? List them here.

Some ministries are there so that people who believe in God can get together and encourage each other as they grow in their understanding of their beliefs. We'll call these Fellowship ministries. Do you know which ones are these? List them here.

Section 3: The church ministers to you

As a member of the church, you will be one part of a large body, both in a Universal Church sense and it a Particular Church sense. How does this work exactly? What part do you have in this body?

Read 1 Corinthians 12:12-31. What does it mean for you to be a "member of the body" as you read about in these verses?

Do you have a particular role, function, or gift which you can use as a part of Christ's body? How are you using it? Discuss this with your parents.

How do you feel like the church ministers to you? In what ways are you not being ministered to by your church? Which do you think is more—the amount you are ministered to, or the amount that you are involved in using your gifts for the church?

Lesson 5 Summary

What is the Universal Church? How do you fit into it?

What is the Particular Church? How do you fit into it?

Name some of the ministries that you know about in our church. What kinds of ministries are those?

How are you involved in ministry in our church? How are you being ministered to by our congregation?

Scripture Memory: 1 Corinthians 12:12

Lesson 6: Getting Down to Business

The Organization of the Church

What does it mean to be "Presbyterian" anyway? Aren't we all Christians? Why do we need a particular name or label like that? How come our church is organized differently from other churches in town?

The organization of the church is sometimes a complicated thing to understand. We have a very specific structure for it, and that structure may seem like it is just a lot of meetings and committees that don't do anything but talk about the same things. But if we look at the reason why we have this structure, and how it functions, we'll see that it does have a good purpose after all. Further, if we look for words about the organization of a church in the Bible, we'll see that the structure our church is using is very Biblical.

Section 1: Our denomination, other denominations

There are basically three different ways that a church can be organized or "governed"—the Episcopal system, the Congregational system, and the Presbyterian system. Let's look at each of those:

Episcopal:

> Churches that are governed in this way have one man, or sometimes a group of men, who makes all of the decisions regarding how the church is to be run; he or they tell the people that are members of the church what they can and cannot do as church members. This man, or group of men, is appointed to the church; the church doesn't get to choose who it will be. Each individual church is a part of a larger group of churches that works the same way—there is a man or group of men that make the decisions for the whole denomination.

Congregational:

> These churches do not have a particular person or group of people who make decisions; instead, everyone in the church gets together and votes on what will happen or what will be done. In these churches, the majority rules! Also, the church may or may not belong to a denomination, but if they do belong to one, the decisions for the denomination are made in the same way-and they do not necessarily affect the churches that are members of the denomination. Each church can choose what it wants—the denomination cannot tell the churches what they should do.

Presbyterian:

> In these churches, the members of the church elect people to lead them and to make decisions. They choose men who they believe will be wise, and who will represent them fairly. Presbyterian churches are also usually members of denominations, and the leaders in the denominations are also elected.

Do you know any churches that operate under the episcopal form of government? How about the congregational? List any that you know below.

Do you know of any institution, besides the Presbyterian Church in America (our denomination), that operates with a presbyterian form of government? Describe that institution here.

Section 2: The officers of the church

When we, as Presbyterians, elect men to represent us and make decisions for us, we say that those men hold an office. Therefore, we call them officers of our church. The officers oversee the spiritual and physical needs of the particular church.

We have two specific offices in the Presbyterian Church in America: the office of Elder and the office of Deacon. Each of these offices has a specific role and function, and we're going to look at those roles in this section.

Elders

Elders are also sometimes referred to as "Overseers." Elders have, as the Book of Church Order tells, duties of "government and spiritual oversight of the church, including teaching." This is a very basic definition; there is a lot that goes into the handling of these duties. Let's look at Scripture to see what it's all about.

Read I Timothy 3:1-7 and Titus 1:5-9. What does the Bible say about the things we should look for in an Elder? Write down a list of these things here.

There are two different kinds of Elders in the church: Teaching Elders and Ruling Elders. In the Presbyterian Church in America we call the Teaching Elders "Pastors." The Bible has specific words about Pastors, in addition to the words about all Elders.

Read I Corinthians 4:1,2 and James 3:1. What does the Bible say that Pastors are? What does it warn about this (in the James verse)?

Why is it so important that we heed the words of the Bible regarding Elders? Discuss this with your parents, and write your thoughts here.

Section 3: The officers of the church, continued...

Deacons

The office of Deacon is also significant in the church; the Book of Church Order describes it as "one of sympathy and service, after the example of the Lord Jesus; it expresses also the communion of saints, especially in their helping one another in time of need." Deacons look after the church in times of need—whether it is someone who is sick, hungry, or homeless. Deacons take care of these needs and more. Let's go to the Bible for insight into the office of Deacon.

Read I Timothy 3:8-13. What are the qualifications of a Deacon? What is different between Deacons and Elders—what duties, qualifications, etc?

Read Acts 6:1-7. Why do we need Deacons—why shouldn't the Elders take care of these needs? Is there a need for both? Write down why, according to the Bible AND according to your thoughts, we need Deacons.

Trustees

The work of our Trustees is also very important, and they too are elected by the church and have the responsibilities for things like buying and selling property for the church, taking care of the buildings and grounds, and general upkeep of all the church properties. The Trustees and the Deacons are all under the authority of the Session (Elders), and the congregation. They manage our funds, and write checks, etc.

Section 4: Church governing and membership

Elders Deacons and Trustees meet regularly— in many churches, they meet every month! The officers of our church are very concerned with overseeing the care, spiritual growth, and activities of the church, and they are very involved in what goes on each week at church.

As you work toward becoming a member of the church, the officers want you to understand how they are at work to oversee the church; they have invited you to attend one of their meetings! At this meeting, you can stay as long as you like, watching what goes on and listening to the discussions. Call the church office to find out when this meeting is.

You'll also have the opportunity to talk with some or all of the Elders about joining the church; If you desire to join the church right away, this will be the time to take the next step in the process (going through this class was the first step). They will want to know about your testimony—you'll be glad that we worked through that a few weeks ago!

If you speak with the Elders and share your testimony with them, then you'll be one step away from being a member of the church! The last step is to stand before the congregation and answer a few questions about what you believe. We'll even tell you the questions ahead of time- in fact, they are listed here:

- ✓ Do you acknowledge yourselves to be sinners in the sight of God, justly deserving His displeasure, and without hope save in His sovereign mercy?
- ✓ Do you believe in the Lord Jesus Christ as the Son of God, and Savior of sinners, and do you receive and rest upon Him alone for salvation as He is offered in the Gospel?
- ✓ Do you now resolve and promise, in humble reliance upon the grace of the Holy Spirit, that you will endeavor to live as becomes the followers of Christ?
- ✓ Do you promise to support the church in its worship and work to the best of your ability?
- ✓ Do you submit yourselves to the government and discipline of the church, and promise to study for its purity and peace?

There they are! By this stage, you should be pretty familiar with what those questions are asking you. If you don't understand one of them for some reason, talk with your parents about it! Once you've answered those questions before the church, you'll be a member of the church! Be proud —this is a significant time for you in your life, one that will have more significance as you grow older.

Lesson 6 Summary

What kind of government does our denomination use? What are the other kinds of church government (define them)?

What are the duties of Elders? What kind of Elders are there?

Why do we need Deacons? How are they different from Elders?

What are the 5 questions you will be asked? Can you answer them all with a "yes"?

Scripture memory: Ephesians 4:14,15

About Doulos Resources

This workbook was written and produced by Doulos Resources, a not-for-profit organization that exists to provide resources to the church and Kingdom for the building up of Christ's body into full maturity and unity.

Doulos Resources is a ministry of pastors, and as such we have prayed for you and your use of this workbook. We trust in the LORD that He has used this book to build you up, guide you in discipleship and learning, and strengthen your understanding and commitment to the church. We pray that He might continue to extend growth and spiritual maturity to you in the days ahead.

If you like this book and would like to learn how to obtain more copies, or if you would like to learn more about the resources and services we provide, please visit us on our website: www.doulosresources.org.